THE STATIONS OF THE CROSS
IN EVERYDAY LIFE

TOWARDS CALVARY

KHOI DOAN NGUYEN MSC

COVENTRY PRESS

Published in Australia by
Coventry Press
33 Scoresby Road
Bayswater Vic. 3153
Australia

ISBN 9780648725121

Copyright © Khoi Doan Nguyen 2019

All rights reserved. Other than for the purposes and subject to the conditions prescribed under the *Copyright Act*, no part of this publication may be reproduced, stored in a retrieval system, or transmitted in any form or by any means, electronic, mechanical, photocopying, recording or otherwise, without the prior permission of the publisher.

Scripture quotations are from the *New Revised Standard Version Bible*, copyright 1989, Division of Christian Education of the National Council of the Churches of Christ in the United States of America. Used by permission. All rights reserved.
Cataloguing-in-Publication entry is available from the National Library of Australia http:/catalogue.nla.gov.au/.

Cover design by Ian James - www.jgd.com.au
Text design by Megan Low (Filmshot Graphics FSG)

Printed in Australia

Contents

Introduction	5
The First Station	10
Jesus prays in the garden of Gethsemane	
The Second Station	12
Jesus is betrayed by Judas and is arrested	
The Third Station	14
Jesus is condemned by the Sanhedrin	
The Fourth Station	16
Jesus is denied by Peter	
The Fifth Station	18
Jesus is judged by Pilate	
The Sixth Station	20
Jesus is scourged and crowned with thorns	
The Seventh Station	22
Jesus bears the cross	
The Eighth Station	25
Jesus is helped by Simon of Cyrene	
The Ninth Station	26
Jesus meets the women of Jerusalem	
The Tenth Station	28
Jesus is crucified	
The Eleventh Station	30
Jesus promises his Kingdom to the good thief	
The Twelfth Station	32
Jesus speaks to his mother and the disciple	
The Thirteen Station	34
Jesus dies on the cross	
The Fourteenth Station	36
Jesus is placed in the tomb	
Concluding Prayer	38
Epilogue	39
When Nothing Stands	

Introduction

Life is not often planned. It usually happens to us rather than how we want it to happen to us. We have no choice or wish for how our life would be and would be like. But despite all that, we do have a vital choice and a freedom given us from within. That is the freedom of responding to what life gives us. That is the choice of how to meet our inevitable and undesirable challenges of everyday events. The practice of the Stations of the Cross is an aid for us to reflect on this choice and freedom in alignment with the choice and freedom of Jesus as he faced his challenges, sufferings and death.

Jesus saves us by his proclamation of the Good News. His proclamation of this Good News includes his active mission and passive mission. His active mission is all his teaching and the signs he worked, focusing on the Reign of God. His passive mission is his passion and death, which are the continuation and culmination of his active mission and in fact his whole mission as the *Abba's* Beloved.

Whatever he has taught and proclaimed by words and deeds, now in his passive mission of proclaiming the Gospel, all this teaching has to be manifested and revealed in his own person. If he has taught so clearly about forgiveness, this is the time to incarnate it in reality. If he has taught meekness and peace, this is when meekness is shown at its best; and peace and reconciliation made for eternity. If he has taught faith and trust in God as our *Abba*, this is the time to hand over his destiny to the Father's loving and forever capable hands. If Jesus' conception in Mary's womb is an expression of the mystery of Incarnation, his life and mission on this earth is an incarnation of the mystery of the Reign of God. And the freedom and the choice Jesus makes in the last moments of his human life are the graced privileges given to those who belong to God's own reign. These are what God wills for us in love.

I first wrote these reflections on the events of Jesus' passive journey during Lent 2018. I wanted to use them in the parish of Our Lady of Rosary, Kensington, NSW, on Good Friday that year. One of my friends in the parish of St Thomas the Apostle, Blackburn, Victoria, heard that I was writing the reflections and asked if she could have a look at them when finished. I shared the reflections with her, and she used them in Blackburn that year. In 2019, both parishes again used the reflections.

Sitting in church in Blackburn, listening again to my reflections read and reflected on Good Friday 2019, I started thinking about putting these reflections to print, so that more people might access them. I have also met people who wanted to have a copy for use in their everyday life.

The more I thought about it, the more I found it true. The story of Jesus' passion and death is not exclusively for Lent or Easter. It is the central story of Christianity; about human life and transformation. It is the story of our everyday life. So this led to the task of editing, writing the introduction and epilogue, adding some of my poetry, and seeking a publisher.

God willing, this is now my gift to others, especially those who are suffering much in life, not knowing what to make of it all, how to deal with what life brings. The reflections are also a gift from my heart when I, too, am having to go through one of the critical times in my life.

Before coming to the story of Jesus' passion and death, allow me begin with a poem I wrote some time last year.

Enough

At times
It's so simple to be so grateful
Grateful for sunshine
Grateful for sunset
Grateful for a quiet walk in the nearby park
Grateful for people I randomly saw on my way
In a coffee shop, in a shopping mall.

Hearing a divine voice singing in the air
Hearing a joy jump out of the heart

For such a simple reason
That I'm alive
That I am who I am.

Life is never enough
When one lives in the shallows
Life can only be known
As more than enough
As an abundant bliss
When one dives into its depth
The depth where one can never touch the ground
Can never feel the bottom
Simply because it has none.

At times it's wonderful to feel grateful
For the whisper in the soul
For poems and songs, books and words
For beauty and artists, love and friendship
For silence to hear and sounds to enthuse.

One can never say enough
To be grateful for unfolding mysteries and endless surprises.
But at times there's no need to say enough
To say thank you
Only to live and experience the sheer gifts
To the very best we can
That's enough

That's gratitude
That's a love responded.

The peace of the Risen Christ be with us always.
Easter 2019

The First Station

Jesus prays in the garden of Gethsemane

Then Jesus went with them to a place called Gethsemane; and he said to his disciples, "Sit here while I go over there and pray". He took with him Peter and the two sons of Zebedee, and began to be grieved and agitated. Then he said to them, "I am deeply grieved, even to death; remain here, and stay awake with me." And going a little farther, he threw himself on the ground and prayed, "My Father, if it is possible, let this cup pass from me; yet not what I want but what you want". (Matthew 26:36-39)

How often do we pray when we are confronted by the challenges of life – sickness, losing a job, losing a friend or a family member, or an accident? What do we do first when these things come to challenge us? Grieving, despairing, resenting, doubting, trying to fight back, trying to mend the problem, trying to remain calm and self-controlled? Jesus, according to the Gospel writer, felt and tried to do all this in the garden of Gethsemane. Jesus felt grieved, even to the point of death. He felt weak in the moment of contemplating his death. He wanted to push it away if he could. Eventually, he put everything into the hands of his loving Heavenly Father, the One he believed always loved him through and through.

The most powerful aspect of Jesus' agony is perhaps not his trust in God but his honesty with God in this critical moment. He was honest in what he felt and what he experienced. Only in this honesty in prayer was he liberated from grief and anxiety, in order to hand back everything to God and keep going on his mission of witnessing to the truth.

Can we be honest with God at the critical moments in our lives? Can we be honest with our loved ones in our vulnerable and weak moments? What happens when we are?

All: Lord, help us in our weakness.

The Second Station

Jesus is betrayed by Judas and is arrested

> *While he was still speaking, Judas, one of the twelve, arrived; with him was a large crowd with swords and clubs, from the chief priests and the elders of the people. Now the betrayer had given them a sign, saying, "The one I will kiss is the man; arrest him." At once he came up to Jesus and said, "Greetings, Rabbi!" and kissed him. Jesus said to him, "Friend, do what you are here to do." Then they came and laid hands on Jesus and arrested him. (Matthew 26:47-50)*

It was a bitter experience for Jesus as he was betrayed by one of his followers. Not only that, but he was betrayed by a kiss – a sign of friendship, intimacy and affection – a kiss that now became a sign of betrayal, handing over the master to the soldiers.

As I was reflecting on this scene, I felt rage and anger towards the person of Judas. I felt bitterness in my mouth, as I think life is sometimes a bit like that. We can be betrayed, even by those closest to us, in the kindest and most generous things they do for us. Behind the masks of kindness and generosity, there are selfish and calculated motives that we might never expect or imagine.

At times like these, we don't know what to do with these people, or how to deal with these situations that would enrage anyone, embitter any heart. In his situation, Jesus still called Judas 'friend' and let him do what he had to do. How many of us can respond the way Jesus did? The point of the Gospel writer is this: Jesus did not repay with anger, rage and bitterness those who chose to betray, reject or even kill him. He received everything that was put on him and transformed it all. When he responded, he responded with grace – meekness and humility of heart.

But there are times when we too betray those who love and care for us. When people betray us, we quickly forget that there is a Judas in each one of us. Perhaps we need to be meek and humble but not foolish and naïve about all the betrayals that happen in life.

All: Lord, help us in our weakness.

The Third Station

Jesus is condemned by the Sanhedrin

Now the chief priests and the whole council were looking for false testimony against Jesus so that they might put him to death, but they found none, though many false witnesses came forward. At last two came forward and said, "This fellow said, 'I am able to destroy the temple of God and to build it in three days.'" The high priest stood up and said, "Have you no answer? What is it that they testify against you?" But Jesus was silent. Then the high priest said to him, "I put you under oath before the living God, tell us if you are the Messiah, the Son of God." Jesus said to him, "You have said so. But I tell you,

> *From now on you will see the Son of Man*
> *seated at the right hand of Power*
> *and coming on the clouds of heaven."*

Then the high priest tore his clothes and said, "He has blasphemed! Why do we still need witnesses? You have now heard his blasphemy. What is your verdict?" They answered, "He deserves death". (Matthew 26:59-66)

As we read the Gospel stories, the writer provides us with an insight into human hearts. In this passage, only the writer knew that the witnesses were making false accusations and that Jesus was innocent. In real life, it is not easy to distinguish between what is true and what is false. I remember a philosopher who once said: "There is only one truth, the truth according to your perception." Jesus was finally condemned for speaking the truth – publically claiming himself to be the Son of Man, seated at the right hand of God. This was a truth that could not be accepted by the religious authorities at the time. Jesus had to die.

Do we often condemn and judge people harshly because they have opposite opinions about things? Are we often quick to make final judgments about people? How successful have we been at playing judges, at playing God? Can we be so sure of the fact that our opinions and perspectives are always right and true?

All: Lord, help us in our weakness.

The Fourth Station

Jesus is denied by Peter

Now Peter was sitting outside in the courtyard. A servant-girl came to him and said, "You also were with Jesus the Galilean." But he denied it before all of them, saying, "I do not know what you are talking about." When he went out to the porch, another servant-girl saw him, and she said to the bystanders, "This man was with Jesus of Nazareth." Again he denied it with an oath, "I do not know the man." After a little while the bystanders came up and said to Peter, "Certainly you are also one of them, for your accent betrays you." Then he began to curse, and he swore an oath, "I do not know the man!" At that moment the cock crowed. Then Peter remembered what Jesus had said: "Before the cock crows, you will deny me three times." And he went out and wept bitterly. (Matthew 26:69-75)

The focus of this scene is Peter. But imagine how saddened Jesus would be when one of his closest disciples, one of his closest friends, denied knowing him at the most critical moment of his life! I am reminded of my own experience, when I was in one of the darkest times of my life. No one was there for me. I was alone, facing the collapse of everything in my life. No one was there. Even one of my closest friends betrayed me by revealing my secrets to others. It hurt and still does.

I am sure you have your own experiences that were to what Jesus experienced.

Peter was a good disciple, even though he denied his master. He had been a close friend of Jesus, and followed him even after he was arrested. But there he was, in the middle of a crowd that was hostile toward Jesus. What could he do in that situation? If he admitted knowing Jesus, he could be arrested and probably condemned too. He was scared and not ready to stand up for what he believed, yet. He would, eventually, but not now.

Perhaps we are all a bit like that. At times we too face the pressure of the crowd, the pressure to be like the majority, so that we are unable to be who we really are. When we deny living our Christian calling, our Christian values in life – that is when we deny Jesus. We are scared to be different – to live differently to others in our families, communities, and workplaces. The scariest thing is not being different. The scariest thing is to be who we really are. Jesus was not afraid to be himself, and that's why he was crucified.

All: Lord, help us in our weakness.

The Fifth Station

Jesus is judged by Pilate

Now at the festival the governor was accustomed to release a prisoner for the crowd, anyone whom they wanted. At that time they had a notorious prisoner, called Barabbas. So after they had gathered, Pilate said to them, "Whom do you want me to release for you, Barabbas or Jesus who is called the Messiah?" For he realised that it was out of jealousy that they had handed him over. While he was sitting on the judgment seat, his wife sent word to him, "Have nothing to do with that innocent man, for today I have suffered a great deal because of a dream about him." Now the chief priests and the elders persuaded the crowds to ask for Barabbas and to have Jesus killed. The governor again said to them, "Which of the two do you want me to release for you?" And they said, "Barabbas." Pilate said to them, "Then what should I do with Jesus who is called the Messiah?" All of them said, "Let him be crucified!" Then he asked, "Why, what evil has he done?" But they shouted all the more, "Let him be crucified!"
So when Pilate saw that he could do nothing, but rather that a riot was beginning, he took some water and washed his hands before the crowd, saying, "I am innocent of this man's blood; see to it yourselves." So he released Barabbas for them;

and after flogging Jesus, he handed him over to be crucified. (Matthew 27:15-24)

The crowd apparently just wanted to kill Jesus, and Pilate was helpless and weak in his authority. He let evil reign over the truth because he was scared of losing his power. But does he really have any power? Even though he was the governor, he could not make his own decisions but allowed himself to be manipulated by the people.

Jesus was not manipulated in his ministry or his mission. Regardless of the demands and expectations of the people he ministered to, he always remained focused on God's will. Doing the loving Father's will identifies who Jesus is.

Look at ourselves. Do we think that we are being manipulated by false voices and pressures – like consumerism, indifference to faith, lack of compassion, hedonism, narcissism, etc.? Do we at times want to judge and condemn people who are generally hated, without any compassion and understanding for them? How can we remain who we are in the midst of social pressures and expectations?

All: Lord, help us in our weakness.

The Sixth Station

Jesus is scourged and crowned with thorns

> *Then the soldiers of the governor took Jesus into the governor's headquarters, and they gathered the whole cohort around him. They stripped him and put a scarlet robe on him, and after twisting some thorns into a crown, they put it on his head. They put a reed in his right hand and knelt before him and mocked him, saying, "Hail, King of the Jews!" They spat on him, and took the reed and struck him on the head. After mocking him, they stripped him of the robe and put his own clothes on him. Then they led him away to crucify him.* (Matthew 27:27-30)

The Gospel writer wants to portray irony in this scene. Jesus was mockingly hailed as the King of the Jews but we, the readers and believers, know that it is true. His Kingship is not about the kind of power that everyone has to bow down to, in fear. The power in the Kingship of Jesus is the power of love which is meek and humble, which is empowering and which liberates people to become who they really are.

The power of love makes people love and not fear one another. All the humiliations the soldiers heaped on Jesus were not of real power but of real fear.

It is when we feel most scared and fearful that we do something harmful to those around us. And often it is because we don't know what to do, because we want to control the situation, or we want to establish our false, selfish selves.

All: Lord, help us in our weakness.

The Seventh Station

Jesus bears the cross

> *After mocking him, they stripped him of the robe and put his own clothes on him. Then they led him away to crucify him. (Matthew 27:31)*

Each one of us has a cross to bear in life. But perhaps one thing to remember is that the cross we have to bear is not necessarily from God. God did not will the cross of Jesus. Instead, Jesus carried the cross designed by the Romans and put on his shoulders by the judgments of the religious and Roman authorities of the day.

What God willed for Jesus, I believe, was that he would fulfil his mission of witnessing to the truth he preached. His preaching of the Good News about the Reign of God needed to continue – to unfold in his confrontation with violent resistance and eventually death.

The cross we bear in our lives today is part of the human condition. Even though God loves us unconditionally, God doesn't necessarily rescue us from our sufferings and challenges. God promises to "redeem" not to "rescue" us. Redemption is very different to rescue or protection. What we often wish for is a life without suffering, without a cross to carry. But we don't often get that.

One thing we might like to keep reminding ourselves – when we carry our cross – is that God is carrying it with us like Jesus was.

All: Lord, help us in our weakness.

The Eighth Station

Jesus is helped by Simon of Cyrene

As they went out, they came upon a man from Cyrene named Simon; they compelled this man to carry his cross. (Matthew 27:32)

Simon was apparently unwilling to help Jesus carry the cross. It would make him look like a condemned criminal, just like Jesus. Would each one of us be willing to be identified with a criminal condemned to death? Would each one of us be ready to be in unity and solidarity with those who are separated, marginalised, discriminated against or labelled as public sinners? Our natural response would be: not really.

Jesus did just the opposite. He dined with sinners; he let sinners come to him; and towards the end of his life, he was judged and labelled as a criminal. No one wanted to be identified with him now. Not Simon of Cyrene, not even his disciples. But the interesting thing is that Jesus did not express any bitterness against the unfairness meted out to him. Jesus was silent in all of this. He kept carrying on.

All: Lord, help us in our weakness.

The Ninth Station

Jesus meets the women of Jerusalem

A great number of the people followed him, and among them were women who were beating their breasts and wailing for him. But Jesus turned to them and said, "Daughters of Jerusalem, do not weep for me, but weep for yourselves and for your children. For the days are surely coming when they will say, 'Blessed are the barren, and the wombs that never bore, and the breasts that never nursed.' Then they will begin to say to the mountains, 'Fall on us'; and to the hills, 'Cover us.' For if they do this when the wood is green, what will happen when it is dry?". (Luke 23:27-31)

Jesus doesn't want to stop the women weeping for him. What the Gospel writer wants to say here is that the real pity should be felt not for Jesus but for those who are crucifying him. Because the harm that they have inflicted upon themselves is much weightier than the physical harm Jesus is experiencing.

There is a truth here. When we do harm to others, we unknowingly inflict harm on ourselves. For example, when we hate someone, the feeling of hatred is nourished and festers in our heart. We lose our heart to this feeling of hatred; we lose our happiness. Or, when we don't want to forgive, we think that we can control or hold those who hurt us responsible. In fact, when we don't know how to forgive, we are held in the prison of the past, the prison of hurt and pain. We are not free.

Those who were killing Jesus were primarily destroying themselves.

All: Lord, help us in our weakness.

The Tenth Station

Jesus is crucified

> *And when they came to a place called Golgotha (which means Place of a Skull), they offered him wine to drink, mixed with gall; but when he tasted it, he would not drink it. And when they had crucified him, they divided his clothes among themselves by casting lots; then they sat down there and kept watch over him. (Matthew 27:33-36)*

There are times in life that we are just like Jesus – being led to places where we would never want to go, tasting vinegar in life's toughness, being stripped of our masks, our safety, our defenses; and finally being crucified, being humiliated, being put down in front of others. Being crucified is when we hit rock bottom in our lives. When we have lost our power, reputation, public face, employment, career, money, investment, families, affections and relationships – things we treasure the most. I do believe that sooner or later, at different stages of life, we all have to experience something like this.

The difference is in how we face our crucifixion. According to Matthew's account, Jesus seems to be silent during his way to the cross as God seems to be silent in people's way to the crosses of their life. But is God really silent in the midst of our life's crucifixions?

Or is God watching over us and waiting to burst into our lives with the transformative powers of the Spirit?
　Are we open to God?

All: Lord, help us in our weakness.

The Eleventh Station

Jesus promises his Kingdom to the good thief

> *One of the criminals who were hanged there kept deriding him and saying, "Are you not the Messiah? Save yourself and us!" But the other rebuked him, saying, "Do you not fear God, since you are under the same sentence of condemnation? And we indeed have been condemned justly, for we are getting what we deserve for our deeds, but this man has done nothing wrong." Then he said, "Jesus, remember me when you come into your kingdom." He replied, "Truly I tell you, today you will be with me in Paradise". (Luke 23:39-43)*

"Jesus, remember me when you come into your kingdom" is one of our favourite responses in the stations of cross. It is interesting that this saying is not from a holy or perfect figure in the Scriptures, nor from one of Jesus' disciples, but from a thief. We often call this thief 'a good thief', but he is still a thief. What is 'good' about him is that he knows what he has done, he accepts the consequences of it, and, moreover, he knows who Jesus is. We can relate with what this thief says probably because we find he closely resembles us. We are just like him, we are sinners.

But can we really be like this thief – knowing and accepting our sins; our wrongdoing and its consequences in our life; and really believing that God always has mercy and abundance of forgiveness for us? So abundant in fact that we can be with Jesus in Paradise today – at any moment that we turn to him.

All: Lord, help us in our weakness.

The Twelfth Station

Jesus speaks to his mother and the disciple

> *Standing near the cross of Jesus were his mother, and his mother's sister, Mary the wife of Clopas, and Mary Magdalene. When Jesus saw his mother and the disciple whom he loved standing beside her, he said to his mother, "Woman, here is your son." Then he said to the disciple, "Here is your mother." And from that hour the disciple took her into his own home. (John 19:25-27)*

In John's Gospel, Jesus begins his earthly ministry by the sign at the wedding in Cana, where his mother plays an important role in urging Jesus to help save the newly wedded couple from the embarrassment of running out of wine at the celebration. She also outlines a model of discipleship by asking the servants to 'Do whatever he tells you', because Jesus is the Word of God. And now at the end of Jesus' earthly ministry, Jesus' mother is there.

Jesus asks the disciple to take his mother home. Taking her home is not only to look after her in her old age but, theologically speaking, it is to contemplate and follow her model as a follower of the Word. Remember what she said at the wedding in Cana: "Do whatever he tells you." Being a disciple of the Word of God, is to listen to the Word and do whatever he tells us in our lives.

Have we really taken Jesus' mother home with us? Have we really followed what she has said: Listen to the Word and then do it?

All: Lord, help us in our weakness.

The Thirteen Station

Jesus dies on the cross

> *From noon on, darkness came over the whole land until three in the afternoon. And about three o'clock Jesus cried with a loud voice, "Eli, Eli, lema sabachthani?" that is, "My God, my God, why have you forsaken me?" When some of the bystanders heard it, they said, "This man is calling for Elijah." At once one of them ran and got a sponge, filled it with sour wine, put it on a stick, and gave it to him to drink. But the others said, "Wait, let us see whether Elijah will come to save him." Then Jesus cried again with a loud voice and breathed his last. (Matthew 27:45-50)*

When death approaches, there are no words that can describe the experience. What Matthew describes in the dying of Jesus is a deep sense of forsakenness that Jesus experienced in his last moments. This last saying of Jesus can be interpreted in different ways, according to Scripture scholars. It could be the beginning of Psalm 23 in which the author begins with a sense of being forsaken by God but finishes the psalm with a sense of triumph and victory in God. It could be a real expression of Jesus' last moment – darkness and isolation.

But in this cry, Jesus still turns to God. In the face of darkness and a deep sense of disconnectedness from his Abba, Jesus still focuses on God.

Can we keep turning back to God when we feel forsaken? A big challenge for all of us is to keep our focus on God in our forsakenness. If Jesus struggled with the feeling of being forsaken, will we not have similar experiences too?

All: Lord, help us in our weakness.

The Fourteenth Station

Jesus is placed in the tomb

> *When it was evening, there came a rich man from Arimathea, named Joseph, who was also a disciple of Jesus. He went to Pilate and asked for the body of Jesus; then Pilate ordered it to be given to him. So Joseph took the body and wrapped it in a clean linen cloth and laid it in his own new tomb, which he had hewn in the rock. He then rolled a great stone to the door of the tomb and went away. Mary Magdalene and the other Mary were there, sitting opposite the tomb.* (Matthew 27:57-61)

Everything seems to be over. It is finished. No more Jesus. His disciples are scattered. All Jesus' efforts seem to die with him and be buried in the tomb with him. In the midst of all this, what strikes me is the presence of Mary Magdalene and the other Mary, who were sitting opposite the tomb. It might be a sign of their mourning Jesus' death. Or it could be that the Gospel writer wanted to portray a sign of waiting?

When everything seems to come to a dead end for us, for God it might be just a beginning. God seems to act when we least expect it, when we can't do anything and are forced to hand everything over to another Power beyond us. I think it is essential to remember this: the mystery of the resurrection is not accomplished by human effort but by God's loving power.

And resurrection can only happen if, in the end, we are willing to hand everything back to God.

All: Lord, help us in our weakness.

Concluding Prayer

Loving and compassionate God, as we journey through life, we know that Jesus is walking with us. As we reflect on Jesus' last journey to the cross, may we be strengthened to follow him in our everyday lives, in the little ways that only you would see and know.

Lord, help us in our weakness and vulnerability. Grace us with patience and forgiveness. Energise us by giving us meaning and value that cannot be measured by worldly success or achievement.

Help us be faithful rather than perfect. Help us be patient rather than judgmental and embittered. Help us be humble rather than selfish and egotistic. Help us be loving as you are always loving to us.

Amen.

Epilogue

When Nothing Stands

*When nothing stands in a storm
The storm that is unexpected and unforeseeable
The storm that takes away precious people and things
The storm that plunges people's hearts and souls
Into darkness and despair.*

*When nothing stands in an earthquake
The earthquake of nature and of evil
The earthquake of expectation and normality
The earthquake of moral standards and human sanity
When nothing stands in a fire
The fire that consumes houses, families and memories
The fire that burns our hopes and dreams
The fire that brings our foundations to testing
The fire that empties all our faith.*

*When nothing seems possible
And love seems at the most powerless place
When life seems no more than meaningless and despair
And energy and enthusiasm seem mere memories
Of a good old time.*

The soul's despairing in darkness
And stuck in the walls of impossibilities and curses
The heart's crying out of tears and desperate prayers
Nothing's a comfort, even just a passing moment
No one's a saviour, even just be a significant friend.

In the deepest of darkness
Grace's touch embraces
In the deepest pit of thought and imagination
Hope's trembling light shines forth unafraid
In the deepest despair of life
Only love prevails and redeems
But never prevent us from suffering and fire.

When nothing can stand
Let's kneel
Asking for help.

This is poem written during Lent one year, at a most despairing moment of darkness and confusion. In earlier times, I often thought that life was wonderful – full of meanings, joys and hopes. But now I see these things as luxuries and I have become poorer than ever, not able to possess anything anymore. I can't even fake it – pretending that I can create them as if they are things I can fabricate at my will.

Meanings, joys and hopes, if true and genuine, are rare, and they are pure gifts. I can no longer seek them but they are given me, in times I never know, in ways I never expect.

In all, God has become to me the strangest lover I have never met. In all, I realise that love is the strangest thing in life that one desires and longs for. Because in seeking it, we will die the death of darkness, isolation and abandonment. All I see is death and the bottom of the grave, but I will never know or even dream of how all this will end. It is the part of God.

www.ingramcontent.com/pod-product-compliance
Lightning Source LLC
Chambersburg PA
CBHW070312010526
44107CB00056B/2573